FOR

BOOK DESIGN BY MULLEN & KATZ

INTERIOR ILLUSTRATIONS COURTESY OF
"THE HERITAGE™ COLLECTION,"
79 FIFTH AVENUE, NEW YORK, NY
10003-3034

Copyright © 1998
Peter Pauper Press, Inc.
202 Mamaroneck Avenue
White Plains, NY 10601
All rights reserved
ISBN 0-88088-067-8
Printed in China
7 6 5 4 3 2 1

CONTENTS

INTRODUCTION

IN THE EARLIEST DAYS OF LITERATURE, POETS AND AUTHORS OFTEN INSCRIBED THEIR WORK WITH THE HOPEFUL INCANTATION, "GO, LITTLE BOOK, GO." AWED BY THE POTENTIAL OF A BOOK TO INSPIRE AND CHANGE THE LIVES OF PERSONS ITS AUTHOR MAY NEVER MEET, THESE FIRST AUTHORS MADE A RITUAL OF WISHING EACH NEW BOOK A LONG AND SAFE JOURNEY OUT INTO THE WORLD. IT IS OUT OF THIS SAME AWE AND RESPECT FOR THE POWER OF WORDS TO TRANSFORM LIVES THAT THIS LITTLE BOOK *BLACK EXCELLENCE* IS OFFERED TO YOU.

IN THESE PAGES YOU WILL FIND MORE THAN JUST EXAMPLES OF BLACK PEOPLE WHO "BEAT THE SYSTEM." HERE YOU WILL FIND THE TESTIMONIES OF COURAGEOUS AFRICAN-AMERICAN WOMEN AND MEN WHOSE ACHIEVEMENTS HAVE HELPED TO

DEFINE NEW STANDARDS OF EXCELLENCE
FOR THAT SYSTEM. THEIR ACCOMPLISH-
MENTS CHALLENGE PEOPLE FROM EVERY
ETHNIC AND SOCIOECONOMIC BACK-
GROUND TO EXCEED AND TO TRANSCEND
THE EXPECTATIONS WE HAVE OF OUR-
SELVES AND OF EACH OTHER.

IT IS MY HOPE THAT YOU FIND IN THESE
PAGES THE SPIRITUAL FUEL TO KEEP YOU
TRAVELING STEADILY IN THE DIRECTION
OF YOUR HIGHEST SELF AND YOUR FINEST
ASPIRATIONS. ALL GREAT ACCOM-
PLISHMENTS FIRST BEGIN AS DREAMS.
HOWEVER, AS A WISE AFRICAN PROVERB
REMINDS US, "NOTHING IS ACHIEVED IN A
DREAM." THEREFORE, USE THIS BOOK TO
FERTILIZE YOUR OWN VISION OF EXCEL-
LENCE, AND THEN LET'S GET BUSY!

S. T.

EXCELLENCE

I WAS RAISED TO BELIEVE THAT EXCELLENCE IS THE BEST DETERRENT TO RACISM OR SEXISM. AND THAT'S HOW I OPERATE MY LIFE.

OPRAH WINFREY,
TALK SHOW HOST, ENTERTAINER,
PHILANTHROPIST

EXCELLENCE IS NOT AN ACT BUT A HABIT. THE THINGS YOU DO THE MOST ARE THE THINGS YOU WILL DO BEST.

MARVA COLLINS,
EDUCATOR

EXCELLENCE IS THE NAME OF THE GAME NO MATTER WHAT COLOR OR WHAT COUNTRY YOU'RE FROM. IF YOU ARE THE BEST AT WHAT YOU'RE DOING, THEN YOU HAVE MY ADMIRATION AND RESPECT.

JUDITH JAMISON,
DANCER AND CHOREOGRAPHER

IF YOU WANT TO BE THE BEST . . . NOT JUST THE *BLACK* BEST OR THE JEWISH BEST OR THE FEMALE BEST OR MALE BEST, BUT THE BEST, PERIOD—YOU'VE GOT TO WORK HARDER THAN ANYBODY ELSE. WHEN YOU'VE SUFFERED AND SWEATED ALL YOUR LIFE AND YOUR TURN COMES UP TO BAT, YOU EITHER SWING AT THE BALL OR BUNT IT. IF YOU WANT TO BE THE BEST, YOU SWING, LIKE ME. THERE'S NOTHING WRONG WITH AMBITION.

SAMMY DAVIS, JR.,
ENTERTAINER

IF ANYBODY CAN DO SOMETHING, YOU CAN DO IT BETTER.

BENJAMIN SOLOMON CARSON,
NEUROSURGEON AND AUTHOR (*ON HOW HIS MOTHER PREPARED HIM FOR SUCCESS*)

BECOMING A
WORLD-CLASS FIGURE
SKATER MEANT
LONG HOURS OF PRACTICE
WHILE SOMETIMES
TOLERATING PAINFUL
INJURIES. IT MEANT
BEING TOTALLY EXHAUSTED
SOMETIMES, AND NOT
BEING ABLE TO DO ALL THE
THINGS I WANTED
TO DO WHEN I WANTED
TO DO THEM.

DEBI THOMAS,
CHAMPION FIGURE-SKATER

WE ALL HAVE ABILITY. THE DIFFERENCE IS HOW WE USE IT.

STEVIE WONDER,
MUSICIAN AND HUMAN RIGHTS ACTIVIST

IF A MAN IS TO BE CALLED A STREETSWEEPER, HE SHOULD SWEEP STREETS EVEN AS MICHELANGELO PAINTED, OR BEETHOVEN COMPOSED MUSIC, OR SHAKESPEARE WROTE POETRY. HE SHOULD SWEEP STREETS SO WELL THAT ALL THE HOSTS OF HEAVEN AND EARTH WILL PAUSE TO SAY, HERE LIVED A GREAT STREETSWEEPER WHO DID HIS JOB WELL.

REV. MARTIN LUTHER KING, JR.,
LEADER OF THE U.S. CIVIL RIGHTS
MOVEMENT, NOBEL PEACE PRIZE RECIPIENT

IT MUST BE BORNE IN MIND THAT THE
TRAGEDY OF LIFE DOESN'T LIE IN NOT
REACHING YOUR GOAL. THE TRAGEDY LIES
IN HAVING NO GOAL TO REACH. IT ISN'T A
CALAMITY TO DIE WITH DREAMS UNFUL-
FILLED, BUT IT IS A CALAMITY NOT TO
DREAM. . . . IT IS NOT A DISGRACE NOT TO
REACH THE STARS, BUT IT IS A DISGRACE
TO HAVE NO STARS TO REACH FOR. NOT
FAILURE, BUT LOW AIM IS SIN.

BENJAMIN MAYS,
MINISTER AND EDUCATOR,
FORMER PRESIDENT OF MOREHOUSE COLLEGE

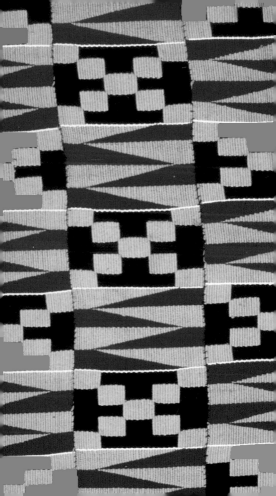

ACHIEVEMENT AND SUCCESS

ADVICE FOR PEOPLE STARTING OUT ON THEIR WAY? IN YOUR MATURITY, TAKE SURVIVAL SERIOUSLY. LEARN TO READ, WRITE, COMPUTE AND THINK. AVOID DRUG CONSUMPTION AND DESTRUCTION OF YOUR BODY AND MIND. AVOID THAT BECAUSE YOU SHOULD BE IN SURVIVAL MODE. . . . AND ONCE YOU'RE PREPARED, YOU NEVER KNOW WHAT ROADS WILL OPEN UP. AND IF YOU'RE PREPARED IT DOES NOT MATTER. IF THERE'S A ROAD YOU CAN PURSUE IT. IF THERE'S NO ROAD, YOU CAN CARVE IT THROUGH BUSHES.

REV. JESSE JACKSON,
POLITICIAN AND ACTIVIST

WHAT ALL ACHIEVING BLACKS SUCCESSFULLY DO IS TURN THE COLOR OF BLACK INTO THE COLOR OF VICTORY.

AUDREY EDWARDS AND CRAIG K. POLITE,
CHILDREN OF THE DREAM

THERE ARE NO SECRETS TO SUCCESS: DON'T WASTE TIME LOOKING FOR THEM. SUCCESS IS THE RESULT OF PERFECTION, HARD WORK, LEARNING FROM FAILURE, LOYALTY TO THOSE FOR WHOM YOU WORK, AND PERSISTENCE.

GENERAL COLIN POWELL,
FORMER CHAIRMAN, JOINT CHIEFS OF STAFF

THE WAY TO BE SUCCESSFUL IS THROUGH PREPARATION. IT DOESN'T JUST HAPPEN. YOU DON'T WAKE UP ONE DAY AND DISCOVER YOU'RE A LAWYER ANY MORE THAN YOU WAKE UP AS A PRO FOOTBALL PLAYER. IT TAKES TIME.

ALAN PAGE,
MINNESOTA SUPREME COURT JUSTICE

JUMP AT THE SUN, YOU MAY NOT LAND ON THE SUN, BUT AT LEAST YOU'LL BE OFF THE GROUND.

AFRICAN-AMERICAN TRADITIONAL SAYING

THERE'S A LOT OF TALK ABOUT SELF-ESTEEM THESE DAYS. IT SEEMS PRETTY BASIC TO ME. IF YOU WANT TO FEEL PROUD OF YOURSELF, YOU'VE GOT TO DO THINGS YOU CAN BE PROUD OF.

USCEOLA MCCARTY,
WASHERWOMAN-TURNED-PHILANTHROPIST

PROBABLY ONE OF THE MOST SERIOUS PSYCHOLOGICAL HANDICAPS YOUNG PEOPLE HAVE TODAY IS THE NOTION THAT IT IS "COOL" TO BE A NON-ACHIEVER, THAT IT IS "HIP" TO PUT DOWN HARD WORK IN SCHOOL.

BILL COSBY,
ENTERTAINER AND PHILANTHROPIST

I THINK IT'S ASININE AND LIMITING TO BUY INTO AN ARGUMENT THAT A LOT OF RACISTS WOULD LOVE TO FOSTER, WHICH IS THAT THE MINUTE YOU CAN ARTICULATE YOURSELF OR THE MINUTE YOU ARE A SUCCESS, THEN YOU ARE SELLING OUT AND TRYING TO BE WHITE. BECAUSE THE CONVERSE IS, IN ORDER TO BE BLACK, YOU MUST BE INARTICULATE AND BE A FAILURE. IF YOU BUY INTO THAT, THEN YOU ALLOW RACISTS TO WIN BECAUSE YOU EITHER CONSIGN YOURSELF TO FAILURE, OR YOU ALLOW YOUR OWN PEOPLE TO TURN THEIR BACKS AGAINST YOU. I THINK IT'S A LUDICROUS ARGUMENT.

BRYANT GUMBEL,
BROADCAST JOURNALIST

I'VE ALWAYS BEEN DRIVEN—BUT I'M NOT THE KIND OF PERSON WHO SAYS "THIS IS GOING TO TAKE ME HERE AND THAT'S GOING TO TAKE ME HERE." I DON'T HAVE GOALS—I HAVE STANDARDS OF ACHIEVEMENT.

ED BRADLEY,
TELEVISION JOURNALIST

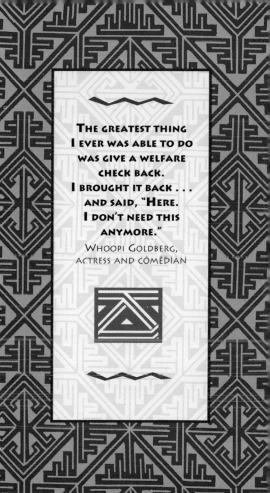

THE GREATEST THING
I EVER WAS ABLE TO DO
WAS GIVE A WELFARE
CHECK BACK.
I BROUGHT IT BACK . . .
AND SAID, "HERE.
I DON'T NEED THIS
ANYMORE."

WHOOPI GOLDBERG,
ACTRESS AND COMEDIAN

I GUESS IF THERE WERE AN EQUATION FOR SUCCESS IT WOULD LOOK LIKE THIS:

PRAY FOR IT + SET IT + WORK LIKE MAD TO GET IT = SUCCESS.

JULIA A. BOYD,
AUTHOR

IF YOU'RE GOING TO REAP THE REWARDS OF SUCCESS, YOU HAVE TO ACCEPT AND LIVE UP TO THE RESPONSIBILITIES IT BRINGS.

EARL G. GRAVES,
FOUNDER AND PUBLISHER,
BLACK ENTERPRISE MAGAZINE

TOO MANY PEOPLE INTERPRET SUCCESS AS SAINTHOOD. SUCCESS DOES NOT MAKE YOU A GREAT PERSON; HOW YOU DEAL WITH IT DECIDES THAT. YOU MUST NOT ALLOW YOUR VICTORIES TO BECOME ENDS UNTO THEMSELVES.

LES BROWN,
MOTIVATIONAL SPEAKER

WORK

I ABOVE ALL BELIEVE IN WORK—SYSTEMATIC AND TIRELESS.

W. E. B. DUBOIS, AUTHOR,
SOCIOLOGIST, ACTIVIST

THE MAN OR WOMAN WHO HAS MONEY, WITHOUT HAVING HAD TO WORK FOR IT, WHO HAS ALL THE COMFORTS OF LIFE, WITHOUT EFFORT, AND WHO SAVES HIS OWN SOUL AND PERHAPS THE SOUL OF SOMEBODY ELSE, SUCH AN INDIVIDUAL IS RARE, VERY RARE INDEED.

BOOKER T. WASHINGTON,
EDUCATOR, ACTIVIST, WRITER

I LEARNED THAT NO MATTER WHAT YOU MAY OR MAY NOT HAVE . . . PEOPLE UNDERSTAND HARD WORK AND TALENT— AND IT CAN PREVAIL.

MAXINE WATERS,
U.S. CONGRESSWOMAN

Work is dignity and caring and the foundation for a life with meaning. For all her great accomplishments, Mary McLeod Bethune never forgot the importance of practical work. When asked by a train conductor, "Auntie, do you know how to cook good biscuits?" she responded, "Sir, I am an advisor to presidents, the founder of an accredited four year college, a nationally known leader of women, and founder of the National Council of Negro Women. And yes, I also cook good biscuits."

Marian Wright Edelman,
founder, Children's Defense Fund

A DREAM DOESN'T BECOME REALITY THROUGH MAGIC; IT TAKES SWEAT, DETERMINATION, AND HARD WORK.

GENERAL COLIN POWELL

DID I PAY MY DUES? YOU BET. WAS IT TOUGH? WITHOUT A DOUBT. BUT I WAS DETERMINED TO FIND OUT HOW HIGH IS HIGH!

HALLE BERRY,
ACTRESS

LUCK IS NICE WHEN IT HAPPENS, BUT IT'S NOT SOMETHING THAT WE CAN COUNT ON REGULARLY. PART OF MY LUCK IS HARD WORK.

JULIA A. BOYD

You just try to do
everything that
comes up.
Get up an hour earlier,
stay up an hour later,
make the time.
Then you look back
and say, "Well that
was a neat piece of
juggling there—school,
marriage, babies,
career."
The enthusiasms
took me through the
action, not the
measuring of it or
the reasonableness.

RUBY DEE,
ACTRESS

MEN MAY NOT GET ALL THEY PAY FOR IN THIS WORLD, BUT THEY MUST CERTAINLY PAY FOR ALL THAT THEY GET.

FREDERICK DOUGLASS,
ABOLITIONIST

IF YOU DO WHAT YOU'VE ALWAYS DONE, YOU'LL GET WHAT YOU'VE ALWAYS GOTTEN.

MOMS MABLEY,
COMEDIAN

YOU HAVE TO STICK TO YOUR PLAN. . . . BUT VERY FEW PEOPLE GET ANYWHERE BY TAKING SHORTCUTS. VERY FEW PEOPLE WIN THE LOTTERY TO GAIN THEIR WEALTH. IT HAPPENS, BUT THE ODDS CERTAINLY AREN'T WITH THEM. MORE PEOPLE GET IT THE HONEST WAY, BY SETTING THEIR GOALS AND COMMITTING THEMSELVES TO ACHIEVING THOSE GOALS. THAT'S THE ONLY WAY I'D WANT IT ANYWAY.

MICHAEL JORDAN,
NBA BASKETBALL SUPERSTAR

WHEN A JOB IS ONCE BEGUN, NEVER STOP UNTIL IT'S DONE. BE THE JOB LARGE OR SMALL, DO IT RIGHT OR NOT AT ALL.

CAROL MOSELEY-BRAUN,
FIRST AFRICAN-AMERICAN WOMAN
U.S. SENATOR

I ALWAYS HAD SOMETHING TO SHOOT FOR EACH YEAR: TO JUMP ONE INCH FARTHER.

JACKIE JOYNER-KERSEE,
OLYMPIC MEDALIST AND TRACK STAR

SELF-RELIANCE

I HAD TO MAKE MY OWN LIVING AND MY OWN OPPORTUNITY. . . . DON'T SIT DOWN AND WAIT FOR THE OPPORTUNITIES TO COME; YOU HAVE TO GET UP AND MAKE THEM.

MADAME C. J. WALKER,
FIRST AFRICAN-AMERICAN
WOMAN MILLIONAIRE

I AM A WOMAN WHO CAME FROM THE COTTON FIELDS OF THE SOUTH.
I WAS PROMOTED FROM THERE TO THE WASHTUB. THEN I WAS PROMOTED TO THE COOK KITCHEN, AND FROM THERE I *PROMOTED MYSELF INTO THE BUSINESS OF* MANUFACTURING HAIR GOODS AND PREPARATIONS.

MADAME C. J. WALKER

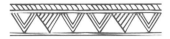

BE READY. BE QUALIFIED. OWN SOMETHING. BE SOMEBODY. THAT'S BLACK POWER.

JAMES BROWN,
ENTERTAINER, "GODFATHER OF SOUL"

MY DADDY USED TO ASK US WHETHER THE TEACHER HAD GIVEN US ANY HOMEWORK. IF WE SAID NO, HE'D SAY, "WELL, ASSIGN YOURSELF." . . . DON'T WAIT AROUND TO BE TOLD WHAT TO DO. . . . HARD WORK, INITIATIVE, AND PERSISTENCE ARE STILL THE NONMAGIC CARPETS TO SUCCESS.

MARIAN WRIGHT EDELMAN

ACCORDING TO THE COMMONEST PRINCIPLES OF HUMAN ACTION, NO MAN WILL DO AS MUCH FOR YOU AS YOU WILL DO FOR YOURSELF.

MARCUS GARVEY,
ORATOR AND POLITICAL LEADER

IT AIN'T NOTHING TO FIND NO STARTING PLACE IN THE WORLD. YOU JUST START FROM WHERE YOU FIND YOURSELF.

AUGUST WILSON,
PULITZER PRIZE-WINNING PLAYWRIGHT

THE LIMITATIONS YOU HAVE AND THE NEGATIVE THINGS THAT YOU INTERNALIZE ARE GIVEN TO YOU BY THE WORLD. THE THINGS THAT EMPOWER YOU—THE POSSIBILITIES—*COME FROM WITHIN.*

LES BROWN

GOD MAKES THREE REQUESTS OF HIS CHILDREN: DO THE BEST YOU CAN, WHERE YOU ARE, WITH WHAT YOU HAVE, NOW.

AFRICAN-AMERICAN FOLK SAYING

IF I HAVE A PHILOSOPHY OF LIFE, IT'S ABOUT MAKING YOUR OWN WAY. GOING OUT AND GETTING IT DONE. NOT EXPECTING IT TO BE DONE FOR YOU.

JANET JACKSON,
ENTERTAINER

CAN'T NOTHING MAKE YOUR LIFE WORK IF YOU AIN'T THE ARCHITECT.

TERRY McMILLAN,
NOVELIST

YOUR WORLD IS AS BIG AS YOU MAKE IT.

GEORGIA DOUGLAS JOHNSON,
POET

WHAT RESONATES FOR ME IS THAT WE NOT SEE OURSELVES AS VICTIMS—THAT WE NOT SEE OURSELVES AS WITHOUT ANY CONTROL OVER IMPORTANT DECISIONS IN OUR LIVES. WE ARE SURVIVORS, NOT VICTIMS, AND WE HAVE TO TAKE A STAND OR TAKE A STEP OR MAKE A STATEMENT THAT ALLOWS US TO MOVE FROM BEING THE VICTIM OF OTHER PEOPLE'S DECISIONS TO THE ARCHITECT OF OUR OWN WELL-BEING AND THAT OF OUR COMMUNITY AND COUNTRY.

LANI GUINIER,
ATTORNEY AND CIVIL RIGHTS ADVOCATE

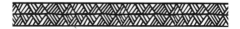

EDUCATION AND LEADERSHIP

JUST *KNOWING* HAS MEANT EVERYTHING TO ME. KNOWING HAS PUSHED ME OUT INTO THE WORLD, INTO COLLEGE, INTO PLACES, INTO PEOPLE.

ALICE WALKER,
PULITZER PRIZE-WINNING AUTHOR

EDUCATION IS OUR PASSPORT TO THE FUTURE, FOR TOMORROW BELONGS TO THE PEOPLE WHO PREPARE FOR IT TODAY.

MALCOLM X,
MINISTER, POLITICAL LEADER,
AND HUMAN RIGHTS ACTIVIST

GIVE YOUR BRAIN AS MUCH ATTENTION AS YOU DO YOUR HAIR AND YOU'LL BE A THOUSAND TIMES BETTER OFF.

MALCOLM X

IT IS ONLY AN EDUCATION THAT LIBERATES. EDUCATION HELPS ONE CEASE BEING INTIMIDATED BY STRANGE SITUATIONS. ONCE YOU HAVE IT IN YOUR MIND, YOU CAN GO ANYWHERE. . . . READ. FIND THAT THERE IS NOTHING THAT IS NOT HUMAN, THAT IF A HUMAN BEING CAN DO THE WORST THING, IT MEANS TOO THAT A HUMAN BEING CAN DO THE GREATEST. HE OR SHE CAN ACTUALLY DARE TO DREAM A GREAT DREAM! AND REALLY CREATE A MASTERPIECE. IF A HUMAN BEING DID IT, THEN OBVIOUSLY I HAVE THAT CAPABILITY OF DOING IT. AND SO DO YOU.

MAYA ANGELOU,
POET AND AUTHOR

NO ONE IS QUALIFIED TO CHANGE THE SYSTEM HE DOES NOT UNDERSTAND. EDUCATION BRINGS THAT UNDERSTANDING.

GEORGE E. JOHNSON,
FOUNDER, JOHNSON PRODUCTS COMPANY

I THINK THAT
EDUCATION IS POWER.
I THINK THAT BEING ABLE
TO COMMUNICATE WITH
PEOPLE IS POWER. . . .
I DO THINK THAT THE
GREATEST LESSON OF LIFE
IS THAT YOU ARE
RESPONSIBLE FOR
YOUR OWN LIFE.

OPRAH WINFREY

ALWAYS BE SMARTER THAN THE PEOPLE WHO HIRE YOU.

LENA HORNE,
SINGER, ENTERTAINER

DO NOT LET YOURSELF BE OVERWHELMED! IF YOU ARE WISE, STRONG ENOUGH TO SURVIVE THE THREATENING ATMOSPHERE OF THE STREETS, THEN CHANNEL THAT SAME ENERGY INTO THRIVING IN THAT SAME ATMOSPHERE AT YOUR SCHOOL.

BILL COSBY

WHILE IT'S GREAT TO BE BLACK AND BEAUTIFUL . . . IT'S EVEN BETTER TO BE BLACK AND BEAUTIFUL AND PREPARED.

MARTINA ARROYO,
OPERA SINGER

NO ONE THAT I'VE RUN INTO FEELS THAT THE DEPTHS THAT I GO INTO ARE NECESSARY. BUT I FEEL THAT JUST HAVING THE NATURAL ABILITY IS NOT ENOUGH. . . . YOU'VE GOT TO READ, LEARN, EDUCATE YOURSELF.

FLIP WILSON,
COMEDIAN

I GREW UP POOR, BUT I DIDN'T KNOW WE WERE POOR UNTIL I MET AFFLUENT PEOPLE IN HIGH SCHOOL. . . . SOMETIMES I WAS ENVIOUS OF OTHERS, OTHER TIMES ASHAMED OF MY POVERTY. BUT WHAT IT REALLY MADE ME FEEL WAS A NEED TO WORK HARD. EDUCATION WAS GOING TO AFFORD ME THINGS.

ANDRE BRAUGHER,
ACTOR

THE ONLY SAFE SHIP IN A STORM IS LEADERSHIP.

FAYE WATTLETON,
SOCIAL ACTIVIST, FORMER PRESIDENT,
PLANNED PARENTHOOD OF AMERICA

I THINK PEOPLE LIKE JULIUS ERVING, DENZEL WASHINGTON, SPIKE LEE, AND MARTIN LUTHER KING—PEOPLE I ADMIRE—ALL CREATED THEIR OWN VISION. . . . THEY SET AN EXAMPLE AND THEY LED. BUT YOU DON'T HAVE TO BE ON TELEVISION, COACH AN NBA TEAM, OR PLAY A PROFESSIONAL SPORT TO BE AN EFFECTIVE LEADER. JUST ABOUT EVERY HOME, EVERY BUSINESS, EVERY NEIGHBORHOOD AND EVERY FAMILY NEEDS SOMEONE TO LEAD. WE'VE GOT ENOUGH PEOPLE TALKING ABOUT IT.

MICHAEL JORDAN

NO MATTER WHERE YOU ARE IN YOUR CAREER OR BUSINESS, THERE IS ALWAYS SOMETHING YOU CAN DO AND SOMEONE YOU CAN HELP IN ORDER TO STRENGTHEN THE ENTIRE BLACK COMMUNITY.

EARL G. GRAVES

ATTITUDE, FAITH, AND DETERMINATION

WHATEVER WE BELIEVE ABOUT OURSELVES AND OUR ABILITY COMES TRUE FOR US.

SUSAN L. TAYLOR,
EDITOR-IN-CHIEF, *ESSENCE MAGAZINE*

THE IMAGE YOU HAVE OF YOURSELF IS IMPORTANT. IF YOU FEEL LIKE A FAILURE, CHANCES ARE YOU'LL FAIL. IF YOU THINK YOU'LL SUCCEED, YOU'LL BE SUCCESSFUL. YOU CAN'T JUST SIT BACK AND EXPECT PEOPLE TO DO THINGS FOR YOU. YOU'VE GOT TO GET UP AND DO IT YOURSELF.

DIANA ROSS,
ENTERTAINER

IT IS THE MIND THAT MAKES THE BODY.

SOJOURNER TRUTH,
ABOLITIONIST AND SUFFRAGIST

I NEVER SAID, "WELL, I DON'T HAVE THIS AND I DON'T HAVE THAT." I SAID, "I DON'T HAVE THIS *YET*, BUT I'M GOING TO GET IT."

TINA TURNER,
ROCK SUPERSTAR

CHAMPIONS AREN'T MADE IN GYMS. CHAMPIONS ARE MADE FROM SOMETHING THEY HAVE DEEP INSIDE THEM—A DESIRE, A DREAM, A VISION. THEY HAVE TO HAVE LAST-MINUTE STAMINA, THEY HAVE TO BE A LITTLE FASTER, THEY HAVE TO HAVE THE SKILL, AND THE WILL. BUT THE WILL MUST BE STRONGER THAN THE SKILL.

MUHAMMAD ALI,
BOXING LEGEND,
FORMER WORLD HEAVYWEIGHT CHAMPION

I HAVE DISCOVERED IN LIFE THAT THERE ARE WAYS OF GETTING ALMOST ANYWHERE YOU WANT TO GO, IF YOU REALLY WANT TO GO.

LANGSTON HUGHES,
POET AND AUTHOR, A KEY FIGURE OF THE HARLEM RENAISSANCE

YOU HAVE TO FOCUS ON WHAT YOU *CAN* DO. THERE ARE PEOPLE WHO CONVINCE THEMSELVES THAT THEY CAN'T DO ANYTHING WITH THEIR LIVES BECAUSE OF WHAT'S HAPPENED TO THEM—AND THEY'RE RIGHT. THEY CAN'T. BUT THE REASON IS THAT THEY'VE TOLD THEMSELVES THEY CAN'T.

WALLY "FAMOUS" AMOS,
ENTREPRENEUR,
CREATOR OF "FAMOUS AMOS" COOKIES

WHETHER OR NOT YOU REACH YOUR GOALS IN LIFE DEPENDS ENTIRELY ON HOW WELL YOU PREPARE FOR THEM AND HOW BADLY YOU WANT THEM. . . . YOU'RE EAGLES! STRETCH YOUR WINGS AND FLY TO THE SKY!

RONALD McNAIR,
CHALLENGER ASTRONAUT

IF PEOPLE AROUND YOU AREN'T GOING
ANYWHERE, IF THEIR DREAMS ARE NO BIG-
GER THAN HANGING OUT ON THE
CORNER, OR IF THEY'RE DRAGGING YOU
DOWN, GET RID OF THEM. NEGATIVE
PEOPLE CAN SAP YOUR ENERGY SO FAST,
AND THEY CAN TAKE YOUR DREAMS FROM
YOU, TOO.

Earvin "Magic" Johnson,
NBA basketball superstar

BEING BLACK DOES NOT STOP YOU. YOU
CAN SIT OUT IN THE WORLD AND SAY,
"WELL, WHITE PEOPLE KEPT ME BACK, AND
I CAN'T DO THIS." NOT SO. YOU CAN
HAVE ANYTHING YOU WANT IF YOU MAKE
UP YOUR MIND AND YOU WANT IT.
YOU DON'T HAVE TO CRACK NOBODY
ACROSS THE HEAD, DON'T HAVE TO STEAL
OR ANYTHING. DON'T HAVE TO BE SMART
LIKE THE MEN UP HIGH STEALING ALL THE
MONEY. WE'RE GOOD PEOPLE AND
WE TRY.

"Mother" Clara McBride Hale,
founder of Hale House,
home for babies of drug-addicted mothers

WHEN TIMES GET TOUGH, REJOICE IN THE
KNOWLEDGE THAT YOU ARE ONE IN A
LONG LINE OF PROUD, COURAGEOUS PEO-
PLE WHO HAVE A HISTORY OF SURVIVING.

DENISE L. STINSON,
AUTHOR

NO ONE CAN DUB YOU WITH DIGNITY.
THAT'S YOURS TO CLAIM. MY FEELING IS,
THE BETTER WE FEEL ABOUT OURSELVES,
THE FEWER TIMES WE HAVE TO KNOCK
SOMEBODY DOWN IN ORDER TO STAND ON
TOP OF THEIR BODIES AND FEEL TALL.

ODETTA,
FOLK SINGER, CIVIL RIGHTS ACTIVIST

AS LONG AS YOU KEEP A PERSON DOWN,
SOME PART OF YOU HAS TO BE DOWN
THERE TO HOLD HIM DOWN, SO IT MEANS
YOU CANNOT SOAR AS YOU OTHERWISE
MIGHT.

MARIAN ANDERSON,
OPERA SINGER, FIRST BLACK WOMAN TO SING
SOLO AT THE METROPOLITAN OPERA

TO BE A GREAT CHAMPION YOU MUST BELIEVE YOU ARE THE BEST. IF YOU'RE NOT, PRETEND YOU ARE.

MUHAMMAD ALI

I'M NOT LIKE YOUR TYPICAL DID-EVERY-THING-THE-RIGHT-WAY-AND-GOT-INTO-MEDICAL-SCHOOL PERSON. I ALWAYS TELL EVERYBODY THAT PERSISTENCE OVERRIDES RESISTANCE.

REGINIQUE GREEN,
PHYSICIAN

I SAW I MADE THE CLASSIC MISTAKES OF A YOUNG FILMMAKER, TO BE OVERLY AMBITIOUS, DO SOMETHING BEYOND MY MEANS AND CAPABILITIES. GOING THROUGH THE FIRE JUST MADE ME MORE HUNGRY, MORE DETERMINED THAT I COULDN'T FAIL AGAIN.

SPIKE LEE,
DIRECTOR AND FILMMAKER

IT DOESN'T MATTER
WHAT YOU'RE TRYING
TO ACCOMPLISH.
IT'S ALL A MATTER
OF DISCIPLINE. . . .
I WAS DETERMINED TO
DISCOVER WHAT LIFE
HELD FOR ME BEYOND
THE INNER-CITY
STREETS.

WILMA RUDOLPH,
OLYMPIC TRACK STAR

SOMETIMES IT TAKES YEARS FOR A PERSON TO BECOME AN OVERNIGHT SUCCESS.

THE ARTIST FORMERLY KNOWN AS PRINCE,
MUSICIAN AND PRODUCER

I FIND THAT IF I'M THINKING TOO MUCH OF MY OWN PROBLEMS, AND THE FACT THAT AT TIMES THINGS ARE NOT JUST LIKE I WANT THEM TO BE, I DON'T MAKE ANY PROGRESS AT ALL. BUT IF I LOOK AROUND AND SEE WHAT I CAN DO, AND GO ON WITH THAT, THEN I MOVE ON.

ROSA PARKS,
CIVIL RIGHTS HEROINE

IF YOU HAVE CONFIDENCE, YOU'LL ALWAYS FIND A WAY TO WIN.

CARL LEWIS,
OLYMPIC TRACK STAR

DON'T DOUBT ME, BECAUSE THAT'S WHEN I GET STRONGER. I LIKE TO SEE THE SMILES ON PEOPLE'S FACES WHEN I SHOW THEM I CAN DO THE IMPOSSIBLE.

MARVIN HAGLER,
BOXING CHAMPION

I BECAME MORE COURAGEOUS BY DOING THE VERY THINGS I NEEDED TO BE COURAGEOUS FOR—FIRST, A LITTLE, AND BADLY. THEN, BIT BY BIT, MORE AND BETTER. BEING AVIDLY—SOMETIMES ANNOYINGLY—CURIOUS AND PERSISTENT ABOUT DISCOVERING HOW OTHERS WERE DOING WHAT I WANTED TO DO.

AUDRE LORDE,
POET AND ACTIVIST

IF YOU BELIEVE YOU HAVE POWER, THAT GIVES YOU POWER, AND IF YOU USE IT, ACT ON IT, YOU CAN MAKE THINGS HAPPEN.

MAXINE WATERS

TOO MANY OF US ARE HUNG UP ON WHAT WE DON'T HAVE, CAN'T HAVE, OR WON'T EVER HAVE. WE SPEND TOO MUCH ENERGY BEING DOWN, WHEN WE COULD USE THAT SAME ENERGY—IF NOT LESS OF IT—DOING, OR AT LEAST TRYING TO DO, SOME OF THE THINGS WE REALLY WANT TO DO.

TERRY MCMILLAN

OPPORTUNITIES
AND OBSTACLES

I SAY LUCK IS WHEN AN OPPORTUNITY COMES ALONG AND YOU'RE PREPARED FOR IT.

DENZEL WASHINGTON,
ACTOR

OPPORTUNITY FOLLOWS STRUGGLE. IT FOLLOWS EFFORT. IT FOLLOWS HARD WORK. IT DOESN'T COME BEFORE.

SHELBY STEFLE,
AUTHOR

REMEMBER, LUCK IS OPPORTUNITY MEETING UP WITH PREPARATION, SO YOU MUST PREPARE YOURSELF TO BE LUCKY.

GREGORY HINES,
DANCER

YOU CAN FOCUS ON THE OBSTACLES, OR YOU CAN GO ON AND DECIDE WHAT YOU DO ABOUT IT. TO ME, IT BREAKS DOWN TO THAT: YOU CAN DO AND NOT JUST BE.

GLORIA DEAN RANDLE SCOTT,
BENNETT COLLEGE PRESIDENT,
FIRST BLACK WOMAN NATIONAL PRESIDENT
OF GIRL SCOUTS OF AMERICA

OBSTACLES ARE NO OBSTACLES. THERE'S ALWAYS A WAY OF GETTING SOMETHING DONE.

JEROME HEARTWELL HOLLAND,
FORMER DIRECTOR,
NEW YORK STOCK EXCHANGE

A HANDICAP ISN'T A HANDICAP UNLESS YOU MAKE IT ONE. . . . WHEN I WAS YOUNG, MY MOTHER TAUGHT ME NEVER TO FEEL SORRY FOR MYSELF, BECAUSE HANDICAPS ARE REALLY THINGS TO BE USED ANOTHER WAY TO BENEFIT YOURSELF AND OTHERS IN THE LONG RUN.

STEVIE WONDER

I TELL KIDS I DIDN'T HAVE THOUSANDS OF DOLLARS TO GO OUT AND RIDE AGAINST THOSE PEOPLE. THEY DON'T NEED IT. DON'T LET THAT STOP YOU. THERE'S WAYS AROUND EVERYTHING. TO THE BROTHER OR SISTER THAT CAN PAINT, GET OUT THERE. LET PEOPLE SEE THAT STUFF, EVEN IF YOU DON'T HAVE THIRTY DOLLARS FOR A PORTFOLIO CASE. GO SOMEWHERE AND LET SOMEBODY SEE THAT STUFF. THINGS HAPPEN. IF YOU WORK ON CARS, IF YOU DO ANYTHING, GET OUT THERE AND DO AS MUCH AS YOU POSSIBLY CAN. MAKE AS MUCH NOISE AS YOU CAN. THAT SQUEAKY WHEEL WILL GET SOME OIL JUST TO STOP IT SQUEAKIN' IF NOTHING ELSE.

CHRISTOPHER EWING,
EQUESTRIAN CHAMPION AND TRAINER

I DO BELIEVE THAT SOME OF THE NEGATIVE THINGS IN MY CHILDHOOD ARE POSITIVE FOR ME NOW. THEY MADE ME WHAT I AM TODAY. I HAD NOT THE HAPPIEST OF UPBRINGINGS, BUT YOU DON'T HAVE TO BECOME A STATISTIC JUST BECAUSE YOU GREW UP IN A BROKEN HOME.

CAROLE GIST,
MISS USA 1990

IT ISN'T WHERE YOU CAME FROM; IT'S WHERE YOU'RE GOING THAT COUNTS.

ELLA FITZGERALD,
JAZZ SINGER

I AM A BLACK WOMAN, THE DAUGHTER OF A PULLMAN CAR WAITER. I AM A BLACK WOMAN WHO EVEN EIGHT YEARS AGO COULD NOT BUY A HOUSE IN PARTS OF THE DISTRICT OF COLUMBIA. I DIDN'T START OUT AS A MEMBER OF A PRESTIGIOUS LAW FIRM, BUT AS A WOMAN WHO NEEDED A SCHOLARSHIP TO GO TO SCHOOL.

PATRICIA ROBERTS HARRIS,
FORMER MEMBER OF U.S. CABINET,
AMBASSADOR, ATTORNEY

DON'T LET ANYTHING KEEP YOU FROM STRUGGLING AND SEEKING TO BE A DECENT, STRIVING HUMAN BEING. IT IS WHERE YOU ARE HEADED NOT WHERE YOU ARE FROM THAT WILL DETERMINE WHERE YOU END UP.

MARIAN WRIGHT EDELMAN

I SEE CHALLENGES, EVEN PROBLEMS, AS OPPORTUNITIES.

DENNIS GREEN,
NFL HEAD COACH

WHATEVER REASON YOU HAD FOR NOT BEING SOMEBODY, THERE'S SOMEBODY WHO HAD THAT SAME PROBLEM AND OVERCAME IT.

BARBARA REYNOLDS,
JOURNALIST

I HAVE LEARNED TO TAKE "NO" AS A VITAMIN.

SUZANNE DE PASSE,
PRODUCER

You can be anything that you want to be, but remember it's not going to be easy. You must work hard, and when things get tough—and they will—and it looks as if you're not going to make it, keep pushing just a little harder. Never give up. Even if you get knocked down you must get back up, because one thing's for sure, you can never beat someone who is willing to go one more round.

Kathy Russell,
Author

WHERE THERE'S A WILL, THERE'S A WAY. IF YOU PROVIDE THE WILL, GOD WILL PROVIDE THE WAY.

BEVERLY BAILEY HARVARD,
ATLANTA CHIEF OF POLICE,
FIRST AFRICAN-AMERICAN WOMAN TO LEAD
A BIG CITY POLICE DEPARTMENT

I ALWAYS HAD ONLY ONE PRAYER: "LORD, JUST CRACK THE DOOR A LITTLE BIT, AND I'LL KICK IT OPEN ALL THE WAY."

SHIRLEY CAESAR,
GOSPEL SINGER

I ALWAYS ASSUMED I WOULD GO INTO SPACE EVER SINCE I WAS A LITTLE GIRL. I WOULD HAVE APPLIED TO BE AN ASTRO-NAUT IF THERE HAD NEVER BEEN A SINGLE PERSON GOING INTO SPACE.

MAE JEMISON,
ASTRONAUT, FIRST AFRICAN-AMERICAN
WOMAN IN SPACE

ROLE MODELS AND LEGACIES

ONE OF THE NEW TERMS IS "ROLE MODEL." WHEN PEOPLE DO NOT WANT TO DO WHAT HISTORY REQUIRES, THEY SAY THEY HAVE NO "ROLE MODELS." I'M GLAD PHILLIS WHEATLEY DID NOT KNOW SHE HAD NO "ROLE MODEL" AND WROTE HER POETRY ANYWAY. I'M GLAD HARRIET TUBMAN DID NOT KNOW SHE HAD NO "ROLE MODEL" AND LED THE SLAVES TO FREEDOM. I'M GLAD FREDERICK DOUGLASS DID NOT KNOW HE HAD NO "ROLE MODEL" AND WALKED OFF THAT PLANTATION IN MARYLAND TO BECOME ONE OF THE GREAT ORATORICAL FIGHTERS FOR FREEDOM.

NIKKI GIOVANNI,
POET

I'D CONTINUE TO TEACH MY CHILDREN WHAT I HAD BEEN TAUGHT: THAT THEY NEEDN'T SEE A BLACK BECOME PRESIDENT OR WIN THE INDY 500 ON TELEVISION BEFORE THEY COULD DO IT IN REAL LIFE.

ERIC V. COPAGE,
AUTHOR AND EDITOR

I RAN [FOR THE PRESIDENCY] BECAUSE SOMEONE HAD TO DO IT FIRST. . . . I RAN BECAUSE MOST PEOPLE THINK THE COUNTRY IS NOT READY FOR A BLACK CANDIDATE, NOT READY FOR A WOMAN CANDIDATE.

SHIRLEY CHISHOLM,
POLITICIAN, FIRST BLACK WOMAN TO
RUN FOR U.S. PRESIDENCY (1972)

I REMEMBER STANDING ALONE AT FIRST BASE—THE ONLY BLACK MAN ON THE FIELD. I HAD TO FIGHT HARD AGAINST LONELINESS, ABUSE, AND THE KNOWLEDGE THAT ANY MISTAKE I MADE WOULD BE MAGNIFIED BECAUSE I WAS THE ONLY BLACK MAN OUT THERE. I HAD TO FIGHT HARD TO BECOME "JUST ANOTHER GUY." . . . BUT I NEVER CARED ABOUT ACCEPTANCE AS MUCH AS I CARED ABOUT RESPECT. . . . I NEVER BELIEVED IN BACKING OUT JUST BECAUSE THINGS WEREN'T THE BEST THEY COULD BE.

JACKIE ROBINSON,
BASEBALL LEGEND, FIRST BLACK TO PLAY
IN THE MAJOR LEAGUES

IT'S NICE TO BE THE FIRST AT SOMETHING. . . . YOU KNOW YOU DON'T HAVE TO WAIT AROUND AND WAIT FOR SOMEONE ELSE TO DO IT. GO FOR IT. JUST BECAUSE SOMEONE ELSE HASN'T DONE IT BEFORE YOU . . . YOU NEVER KNOW, YOU MIGHT HAVE WHAT IT TAKES TO BE THE FIRST.

CAROLE GIST

WHEN OUR . . . HEROES
ARE PORTRAYED AS
BIGGER THAN LIFE,
LIVING, WORKING,
ACCOMPLISHING BEYOND
THE REALM OF THE
NORMAL, WHEN THEY ARE
DEPICTED AS PERFECT
HUMAN BEINGS . . . THEY
ARE PLACED SO FAR FROM
US THAT IT SEEMS
IMPOSSIBLE THAT WE
COULD EVER TOUCH THEM
OR MIRROR WHO THEY
ARE IN OUR OWN LIVES.

JOHNNETTA COLE,
FIRST BLACK WOMAN
PRESIDENT OF
SPELMAN COLLEGE

MY EXTRAORDINARY PARENTS WERE THE BEST HUMAN BEINGS . . . THEY TAUGHT ME AND MY BROTHER HOW BLESSED WE ARE TO BE BORN AMERICANS WHERE OPPORTUNITIES ARE ABUNDANT.
THEY INSTILLED IN US THE DESIRE AND DRIVE TO BE THE BEST AT OUR CHOSEN GOALS AND ALTHOUGH OUR PATHS MAY PROVE DIFFICULT AT TIMES, TO ACCEPT THE CHALLENGES AND REMEMBER THAT ACCOMPLISHMENTS HAVE NO COLOR; THAT A MOUNTAIN CAN NEVER BE CLIMBED SUCCESSFULLY LOOKING DOWN, THE DIRECTION SHOULD ALWAYS BE ONWARD AND UPWARD, AND WITH FAITH, FOCUS, DISCIPLINE, DEDICATION AND HARD WORK, OUR DREAMS WILL BE REALIZED.

LEONTYNE PRICE,
OPERA SINGER

WE GREW UP IN A GENERATION WHERE PEOPLE WERE CONCERNED ABOUT WHAT YOU WERE GOING TO BE, BECAUSE THE RACE NEEDED YOU. WE WERE REARED TO BELIEVE A SINGLE FAILURE WAS ONE THAT WE COULD NOT AFFORD. I HOPE WE CAN REGAIN THAT URGENCY.

BISHOP LEONTINE KELLY,
FIRST AFRICAN-AMERICAN FEMALE BISHOP,
METHODIST EPISCOPAL CHURCH

I WAS THE ONLY NEGRO WOMAN IN MY DENTAL SCHOOL CLASS, AND I WAS MIGHTY LONELY, BUT I DIDN'T LET THAT STOP ME. I WANTED TO BE THE BEST DENTIST THAT EVER LIVED. PEOPLE SAID, "BUT SHE'S A WOMAN; SHE'S COLORED," AND I SAID, "HA! JUST YOU WAIT AND SEE."

BESSIE DELANY,
DENTIST AND AUTHOR

"I'm going to give you some free advice: Early to bed, early to rise, work like a dog and advertise!" . . . That was my father's way of telling me I had to learn to do it for *myself*; that he loved me enough not to allow me to ride on his success by doing it for me. Though it didn't seem like it then, it was the greatest gift he could have ever given me. So many kids of famous people never learned the value of *earning* something, or how sweet it is to have accomplishments to call your own.

Mario Van Peebles,
Actor and director

I AM A PRODUCT
OF EVERY OTHER BLACK
WOMAN BEFORE ME
WHO HAS DONE OR SAID
ANYTHING WORTHWHILE.
RECOGNIZING THAT
I AM A PART OF
THAT HISTORY IS WHAT
ALLOWS ME TO SOAR.

OPRAH WINFREY